Inside The Broken Mind

Megan Tsiotsios

BookLeaf Publishing

Presentation by *BookLeaf Publishing*

Web: www.bookleafpub.com

E-mail: info@bookleafpub.com

ISBN: 9789357616881

First edition 2022

There are so many people that deserve to be the first dedication to my first ever completed book of solely my poetry, but alas there can be only one. I dedicate this book to my Nanna, Tup Tup, my fierce protector and one of my favourite people in the world. I wish that I had been brave enough to do this before you passed away, but I'm sure that you were the extra nudge I needed to get across the line.

ACKNOWLEDGEMENT

I would like to acknowledge my family. Without my family I probably wouldn't be here today. Without my children to fight for everyday and the unwavering support from my parents when things get tough, without my husband to bounce ideas off and to talk me down when the world gets too much I would be eternally lost. Thank you all from the bottom of my heart.

PREFACE

This book came into being after I saw an advertisement about #TheWriteAngle Writing Challenge and I said to my husband about it. Our 11 year old grandson overheard me and said "you should do it Nanny." So here it is...

A poem for Tup Tup

When I was a little girl,
You were my Nanna Tup.
Until your great grandson was born,
Then he shortened it to Tup Tup.

You have had a huge impact on my life,
And the lives of both of my children.
For that I could never thank you enough,
You were definitely one in a million.

Tonight I lay my head down,
And my heart begins to break.
Because I know when I wake up,
Your smile isn't here to take.

You fought so hard to be here,
To not leave us behind.
But we understand the fight was hard,
In the end you weren't unkind.

I couldn't ask for a better nanna,
I have always known your love.
I will continue to know it though,
Now it will just come from above.

You told us all you loved us,
And you told us not to cry.
Now you will be the sparkling star,
That will always catch my eye.

I am like the wind

I am like the wind blowing through the trees,
Angry and lashing out.
I am like the wind blowing through the trees,
With no real direction.
I am like the wind blowing through the trees,
Not knowing which way to turn.
I am like the wind blowing through the trees,
Wild and scared and haunted.
I am like the wind blowing through the trees,
Just looking for a place to belong.
I am like the wind blowing through the trees,
Soon to be exhausted.

I wish that I could show you

I wish that I could show you how wonderful you are,
How strong you are inside and that you will of course go far.
Your life will be so much better than you could ever have believed,
So please don't let the struggle now leave you feeling so aggrieved.

I wish that I could show you how proud of you I am,
That you manage to keep on going even when you're in a jam.
Your hard work and dedication is something to be admired,
There are so many people in your life that you have definitely inspired.

I wish that I could show you just where you will end up,
When everything seems too hard and you want to just give up.
The future laid before you is shining really bright,

Look at the end of the road, can you see the
shining light?

I wish that I could show you that the hard work
is almost through,
That the reprieve that you are craving is almost
into view.
An end of the years of struggle, they were
almost too much to bear,
When you felt that you were drowning, now you
can come up for some air.

I wish that I could show you that everything will
be alright,
Because you put the effort in regardless of how
hard the fight.
The days of struggle are almost over and the day
of reward awaits,
You will finally get to find the time to hang out
with your mates.

I wish that I could show you how special you are
to me,
Because then you would feel much better, if you
could only see.
The smile you place upon my heart when my
days are also bad,
The fact that I get to call you my daughter
makes me really glad.

I wish that I could show you how brightly your light does glow,
Then you finally would believe me that this is actually so.
I know at times you struggle to see the worth within yourself,
But your worth could fill a hundred books upon the tallest shelf.

I wish that I could show you just how much you mean to me,
That I could take away your stress so that you could be free.
Always remember our days are numbered there's no promise of one more,
Never forget you are my special girl, the one that I adore.

Bipolar

Inside my head is a constant scream,
Just wanting to be let out.
A scream of anger? frustration? maybe,
I'm not sure what it's all about.
The noise in my head is never ending,
There is rarely any real respite.
Even when I'm busy it is there,
Even worse when I turn out the light.
As I lay in the darkness in bed,
Praying for sleep to come.
The scream gets even louder,
And my emotions start to numb.
This is the scariest time of all,
When I feel absolutely nothing.
I try to stay upbeat and smile,
But my brain knows that I'm bluffing.
The numbness is all consuming,
Like being swallowed up by a void.
I cannot cry, I cannot smile,
The depression, once again deployed.
Most days when I open up my eyes,
I know almost at once.
The type of day I'm going to have,
Some days my depression hunts.
Other days when I am manic,

I feel I'm on top of the world.
I open my eyes and think "oh no,"
My emotions are set off and swirled.
Some days the smallest of things,
Leaves me feeling so annoyed.
And I cannot let things go unsaid,
So an argument I can't avoid.
Most days I am exhausted,
Sometimes with the smallest of tasks.
Tired of my bipolar brain and life,
And of everything that it asks.

When my soul lies bare and bleeding

When my soul lies bare and bleeding,
And my words are a constant pleading.
This is the time I need you the most.

When my soul lies bare and bleeding,
And my thoughts of you are fleeting.
This is where you need to make yourself heard.

When my soul lies bare and bleeding,
And my contempt for you is breeding.
This is where I must remember to breathe.

When my soul lies bare and bleeding,
And I cannot stop the eating.
This is where I need you to be my control.

When my soul lies bare and bleeding,
And my depression just keeps on peaking.
This is where I need you to hold me.

When my soul lies bare and bleeding,
And I feel your love is leaving.
This is where I need you to not give up.

Changing tides

Some days I hate my life almost as much as I hate me,
I wake up disappointed, once again, I am not free.
I wish that I could be someone that doesn't have bipolar,
Instead of always feeling like I've been hit by a steamroller.
Every day I struggle with my brain fighting with itself,
The one thing that you cannot hide from is of course ones self.
Every time I look in the mirror, I hate what's reflected back at me,
I know I should have more self worth but I do not hold that key.
Most days I put on my big girl pants and just go through the motions,
My moods change so frequently, like changing tides of the largest oceans.
Some days I start off happy and I think that the day will go well,
But then the wind changes and my depression starts to swell.

Next minute I am angry and annoyed by all that
surrounds,
People, places, sometimes smells, or just the
smallest sounds.
I drive my family crazy with the horrible mood
swings,
If only I finally could control these stupid, crazy,
things.
I have so many things in place, to keep me on
the path,
But I have so many bad days still, that I wish I
could just halve.
For in this life this is the card that has been dealt
to me,
Maybe in my next life the new card will mean
I'm free.

A little bit of hope

A little bit of hope can help you hang on through the day,
It can help you see more clearly and help you move on from dismay.
A little bit of hope can help you see the path ahead,
Instead of the despair that leaves you wishing you were dead.
A little bit of hope can help you tackle all the tasks,
That seem to be unending and seem way too much to ask.
A little bit of hope can help you get up out of bed,
To help you follow up on promises that keep running through your head.
A little bit of hope can always go a real long way,
When all the roads feel blocked hope helps you find a simple way.
A little bit of hope can make the sunshine break on through,
It also helps you realise that there is plenty still to do.

A little bit of hope can make you feel all is
alright,
It can help to open up your eyes and make you
stand and fight.
A little bit of hope can help to pull you from
your rut,
It can help you hit depression with a killer
uppercut.
A little bit of hope is the only thing you need,
To make you keep on fighting and help you to
succeed.

Sunshine

They tell me to get out into the sunshine,
That it will make everything feel better,
And even though I know that's true,
I don't feel like being a go-getter.
I want to curl up in a ball,
And never go outside,
There are far too many people out there,
I'd rather stay inside and hide.
But I sit at my bedroom window,
With the curtains pulled all the way up.
And I can't help but be seduced,
By the sun that has just come up.
It warms my face and makes me smile,
It makes me very slowly get up.
I throw on a loose fitting T-shirt,
And a pair of leggings or jeans.
Then I put my runners on my feet,
The puppy starts jumping, full of beans.
She knows just what I'm doing,
That we are going to venture outside.
We're going to get out into the sunshine,
We are not going to stay and hide.
We step outside and take a deep breath,
Inhaling the freshly mowed grass.
The smells of summer are carried on the breeze,

The sunshine is really first class.
I feel it soaking into my skin,
Lighting my mood just like a candle.
I know when I'm walking in the sun,
That there is nothing that I can't handle.

My little boy

Once you were my little boy,
Who sat upon my knee.
Now you are my little boy,
Who stands much taller than me!
It doesn't matter how old you get,
I will always be your mum.
You will always be my little boy,
And always my favourite son.
You have grown into a man,
That has made me super proud.
Smarter than most your age,
You have never followed the crowd.
Even though you spend most of your time,
Hidden away inside your room.
I love it when you come outside,
Because that's when I see you bloom.
You have a vast knowledge of many things,
Of subjects I know nothing about.
But you never make me feel stupid,
You just explain and help me out.
You have always been generous,
With all you have to share.
Always my ray of sunshine,
With your glorious head of hair.
Any time I need some help,

You always lend a hand.
You'll always be my little boy,
Even though you are now a man.

Meandering along the bush track

One of my favourite things to do,
Is to get lost all by myself,
Meandering along the bush track.

The dappled sunlight streaming through,
I am lost within my thoughts,
Meandering along the bush track.

Listening to the bird song,
Watching them flit and flutter by,
Meandering along the bush track.

The smells of all the flora,
And the ocean on the breeze,
Meandering along the bush track.

The dusty, potholed walking trail,
The branches that snag my shirt,
Meandering along the bush track.

My quiet place of solitude,
My little piece of Heaven,
Meandering along the bush track.

Haunting Memories

I wish that I could turn off,
All the memories in my brain.
The constant flickering images,
Slowly driving me insane.
The nights I lay here were lonely,
Because you were not here with me.
The reason that you weren't here,
Just will not leave me be.
The memories of the heartbreak,
The constant feeling of betrayal.
Every time I think of us,
I wonder if we're bound to fail.
Some days I feel like we are fine,
There's nothing we can't overcome.
But then we have a few rough days,
And I feel my optimism was dumb.
I feel as though these memories,
Are on an endless torture loop.
I close my eyes and see the messages,
Hear the words and I feel like a dupe.
My dream is these haunting memories,
Leave me in peace for once and for all.
I am so over this horrid feeling,
From when my heart was in free fall.

Missing you

I miss your little faces,
And your happy little laughs.
The nights we spent together,
Are captured in photographs.
It feels like so long ago,
That I held you in my arms.
I never thought that loving you,
Could do you so much harm.
They say it takes a village,
To raise a single kid.
But you were taken from our village,
Your parents took you from us and hid.
We went from seeing you weekly,
Now it has been almost nine years.
Since we have seen your little faces,
Or helped wipe away your tears.
You have missed so many occasions,
That the family have spent together.
I wish that we could have you back,
But I fear that day will be never.
You have not seen your cousins,
Some you have never even met.
So many missed experiences,
That you will never ever get.
From sitting around the fire,

In Nanna and Granddad's yard.
From going to the farm at Kath's,
Without you there it is always hard.
I wish that I could change things,
To make everything alright.
But I know that that would only cause,
Yet another pointless fight.
I hear I have a new nephew,
That I know I will never see.
But the thing I wish for most of all,
Is that you haven't forgotten me!

A poem for my husband

I want to take this time out,
To put pen to paper for you,
To tell you how much you mean to me,
As it's something I rarely do.
Even though I often think about,
How much love I have for you.
I just seem to take it for granted,
That it was something that you just knew.
I know at times things have been rough,
And not always an easy ride.
But I guess we needed to hit rock bottom,
In order for us to glide.
In 20 years you have become,
An important part of my life.
My favourite memory together I have,
Isn't the day I became your wife.
Instead it's the time we spent in Lakes,
The year you proposed to me,
Our days spent fishing, swimming and drinking,
Around the fire happy and free.
The days when times were simple,
Where there wasn't very much fuss,
Even though with kids and pets and jobs,
There has never been just us!
Through all the ups and downs,

There has always been one thing.
That's always kept us strong,
No matter what this crazy life brings.
And that one thing has been the love,
That has scorched both of our souls,
That kept burning for the two of us,
Regardless of life's tolls.
I couldn't think of anyone,
I'd like to spend my life with more,
I will love you till the end of time,
And forever more.

Rain

Laying in bed listening to the constant rhythm of the rain,
Drip, drip, wash away my sorrow,
Drip, drip, wash away my pain.

Hearing the raindrops fall, running down my windows, bouncing off my roof,
Drip, drip, wash away my loneliness,
Drip, drip, of my hurt there is no proof.

Knowing the misery is temporary doesn't console me,
Drip, drip, washing my soul clean,
Drip, drip, helping me be free.

Freedom from society's belief of what's right and what's wrong,
Drip, drip, the rain makes me smile.
Drip, drip, because it reminds me I am free.

Free to run wherever I wish, follow my own path like the raindrops,
Drip, drip, my happiness is growing,
Drip, drip, free like the rain, I AM ME!

Insignificant and small

Nothing makes you feel more insignificant and small,
Than sitting on the beach shoreline and watching the winter squall.
It has a way of washing away the stress and worries from your mind,
When the troubles flare up inside my head I try to remember to be kind.
When my thoughts have run away with me and they become so twisted and dark,
That's when I pick myself up and head to the nearest park.
I know that things are really bad when the park just doesn't do,
So I head down to the nearest beach and sit and watch the view.
There's something about the salt in the air and the waves crashing to shore,
That helps to lift my darkest clouds and helps my moods to soar.
The only time I like to feel insignificant and small,
Is when I'm all alone and sitting on the soft and sandy shore.

Inside a broken mind

Inside a broken mind everything is fractured, I
can't work out which was is up or down.
Inside a broken mind nothing makes sense,
sometimes there's fear sometimes there's nothing
at all.
Inside a broken mind thoughts fly free and with
abandon, so many emotions; happiness, sadness,
anger and hate.
Inside a broken mind the constant scream is
loud, I am unable to turn the volume down.
Inside a broken mind the constant scream is
loud, I am unable to turn the volume down.
Inside a broken mind there is no escape, no
words of kindness or tenderness help.
Inside a broken mind no calmness is found,
everything is messy and all over the place.
Inside a broken mind my soul tears itself apart,
trying to find some equilibrium in order to
survive.
Inside a broken mind is a scary place to be, so
much terror and the daily tortures reside.
Inside a broken mind I search for the elusive
calm, somewhere to find some quiet from the
raging storm inside.

Inside a broken mind freedom cannot be found, there is no such thing as calmness or quietude in here.
Inside a broken mind I am always so alone, except for the screams and never ending swirling emotions.
Inside a broken mind I slowly start to unravel, I have fought so hard for so many years.
Inside a broken mind I feel isolated in a room full of people, at best it's like standing in the eye of the storm watching the emotions change.
Inside a broken mind everything feels hopeless and dark, I just want to give up and sleep for a while.
Inside a broken mind you aren't even safe when you sleep, the nightmares continue whether you are awake or asleep.
Inside a broken mind it's hard to go on each day, people don't understand, they can't, their mind is not fractured.
Inside a broken mind there is so much confusion even though all looks to be controlled, nothing is really controlled it's just easier to fake it.
Inside a broken mind...

A childhood of dreams

I have heard so many people talk of troubled childhoods,
But I am one of the lucky ones for my childhood was good.
Some would say that mine has been a childhood of dreams,
The more I speak to others this is exactly what it seems.
My parents are the best parents that anyone could ask for,
Nothing is too much to ask, my parents just keep giving more.
Our Christmas days were extravagant, so many presents under the tree,
But the gifts always came second place if you ever had asked me.
The love from both my parents was never ever once in doubt,
And if ever we were in any trouble mum and dad would help us out.
So many wonderful memories of all the time we spent together,
Our weekends were so full we couldn't say we were bored ever!

Walking through the Brisbane Ranges or hiking the vast You Yangs,
Making rockets in the shed with dad there were always lots of bangs.
So many sporting events, cricket and basketball to name a couple,
I'm sure my parents wished instead of two that they were doubled.
Our childhood birthday parties made us the envy of our friends,
So much food and many games that we wished they didn't end.
We are all adults now and we have children of our own,
But walking into mum and dad's is knowing we are home.
The support we had from our early days right up to our adulthood,
Is something that you have to wait until you're older to be understood.
I wish that I could repay my wonderful parents for my raising,
But there are not enough words other than to tell them they are amazing.

Bestest Boy

The first little boy to call me Nanny,
That swelled my heart with joy,
It was my lovely Brody Kyle,
From the start, my bestest boy.
You are an old soul beyond your years,
On your shoulders you carry the world.
But from the moment that I met you,
My love for you unfurled.
Your love of everything with wheels,
Makes your Pa and I really smile.
Your knowledge of mechanics,
Could go on for many miles.
I cannot wait to watch you grow,
And see all you will become.
I'm sure you will reach many goals,
And along the way have fun.
I love the time we spend together,
Making arts and crafts and reading.
Watching your confidence grow,
For me it is really very pleasing.
Every time I see you,
It seems that you have changed.
Besides from getting taller,
In your maturity you have aged.
The little boy that followed me,

Is growing up too fast.
But regardless of how old you are,
My love for you will always last.
You'll always be my bestest boy,
From now until forever.
The special bond that we have,
Will never end, not ever.

Grandma

You are the last of my six grandparents,
To sadly pass away.
But I have so many memories of you,
To help me through the day.
From helping pick the veggies,
From your little veggie patch.
Shelling peas on the back step,
The ones I ate you didn't catch.
Lovingly tending to the garden,
And pulling out the weeds.
I think my love of gardening,
Came from you planting all those seeds.
You finally taught me how to knit,
A bag of pink and black.
So much frustration though,
I certainly never went back!
From walking into town,
Sitting inside your shopping jeep.
If I was a good girl,
We'd stop and get a treat.
I remember staying at the shack,
And playing backgammon and cards.
I remember my first taste of yabby,
And spending time in the dusty yard.
My love of old time movies,

I definitely got from you.
Meet me in St. Louis,
And Casablanca to name a few.
Eating dinner with steamed cabbage,
And your yummy homemade chips.
Going on holidays to Lakes Entrance,
Sometimes felt like a very long trip.
Days spent sitting in the tree,
Reading books in your front yard.
Saying goodbye to you,
Has definitely been hard.
I'm glad you enjoyed the music,
I recorded for you to hear.
Whenever I listen to it now,
I can still feel you are near.
But I'm glad you are no longer trapped,
In a body that gave up on you.
I'm glad your brilliant mind is free,
And thankfully you are too.

The fire of depression

Sitting watching the fire,
And I slowly begin to laugh.
The flames, like my depression,
Destroy everything in its path.
Dancing naked above the flames,
Sometimes I'm soaring high and free.
But as I begin to sink lower down,
The red hot flames devour me.
I fight with all I have to fight,
But this feeling won't let me be.
Depression once again takes hold,
Then my salvation I cannot see.
As the hot coals start to smoulder,
And turn to cold black lumps of coal.
My mind starts to race inevitably,
And I wonder if I will ever feel whole...

The light will always come

Some nights are dark and then they just keep getting darker,
Then just when you feel like it's time to give up the light starts to creep in at the edges.
It doesn't matter how dark it gets, the light will always come,
Sometimes it feels like it's gone and it's never coming back.
But it's already there if only you could look past your troubles,
Your fears and your depression.
From the stars that sparkle in the sky,
If only you would look up.
To the little indicator light on the television,
Or on your phone that's charging.
Always look for the light,
The light will always come.
You can always find a source of light,
Regardless of how small or dim that light is.
Even if you are the one that has to take control,
Turn on the light yourself, do it.
You can always find the light,
Even if help from others is needed in order to do so.
I understand the dark days all too well,

They are horrendous and seem unending.
But I promise they do not last forever,
There will only ever be 24 hours in a day.
All you need to do is survive them,
You have survived all the other dark days.
You will survive the ones that are still to come,
As long as you remember that the light will always come.
The light will always come.

www.ingramcontent.com/pod-product-compliance
Lightning Source LLC
Chambersburg PA
CBHW062203160726
48282CB00027B/979
9789357616881